LOVE

by

Dikachi Mann

Author contact;

http://www.amazon.com/Dikachi-Mann/e/B015G6U6BU

https://www.facebook.com/DikachiMann/

Preface

Love offers us many opportunities as well as challenges. These two factors make love and loving worthwhile; they both come to unveil our potential and love's many profound truths that we otherwise would never have come upon! So we should never disdain or shy away from them! I for one have learnt this from several of my personal life experiences on the subject in my few decades on earth. And yes! Heartbreak and hurt are constant hazards of love, but should never stop or conquer love!

Over several months, I carefully documented what would otherwise be the deepest life changing lessons I learnt on my journey of love. Thirty-one of those lessons are carefully distilled in this book as quotes. On the surface, these quotes are helpful and applicable to daily life, however, if you read just one a day and spend time mulling over it through the day, you will discover it will help you unveil an answer to one of your conundrums of love. An answer that lay before your eyes, but you never could comprehend or see before! How? The human mind works in such a way that once it is rightly focused it can solve any problem it sets to resolve.

This book gives you that focus which you require.

As you read these quotes, I believe these words will not just be the light to help you on your daily life's path, but also a ready companion in times of despair.

I also encourage you at the end of this book to come up with a personal declaration, which will become your own personal mantra to love every day.

I bid you Godspeed as you begin your transformational journey to truly LOVE!

Acknowledgements

I am thankful for the life circumstances that brought me to the point of writing this book. And also owe thanks to the individuals who have taken part in my life's story so far, most especially my family, loved ones and friends, who made the journey bearable.

I would not be who I am today without you.

Thank you!

Dikachi Mann,
12th January 2016.

Love begins……

Love is more meaningful and much easier to experience, and enjoy when you have the right perspective.

What's your perspective of love?

Love happens…..

But you ultimately decide what happens next.

Love is not an emotion!

To love another being is perhaps one of life's greatest tasks.

If it does not senselessly consume you, it is not love…..for love consumes you to live!

Love speaks very few words in comparison to its actions.

Love is infinity……Infinity is love!

It is disastrous to awaken love when you are not ready for it!

Where there is love, there is no strife!

Faithful are the wounds of love,

For in its healing we find strength!

You can never truly know how to love yourself until you have loved another.

This is the irony of love!

Those who love deepest are often those with the deepest scars, yet the most fortunate of all humanity to have loved!

Music and a retinue of colors simply emanate from the earth,

When your lover tells you no silly words,

Nor spins you lengthy yarns….

But just loves you….

Just as….you are!

There is no singular qualification with which to measure love.

Love is simply what two individuals make of it.

Love purifies the heart,

Frees the soul,

And gives hope for a better tomorrow.

Love is often at war with popular opinion!

Like the transition of a caterpillar, loves changes you….

Love sets you free!

Consider it not, if it hath not love at its core!!

***A** sure recipe for disaster, hurt and regret, is to direct your love at what is at best fleeting!*

It is wisdom to understand this….

Sex is not love, neither is love sex!

Never confuse them for one and the same thing.

There is no love without self-denial, for in love....

Self.......ceases to exist!

Choose wisely whom you decide to love,

It will ultimately determine your life's priorities!

Love is patient, kind, and eternal.

But love also knows when to forgive and let go.

***B**y all means love deeply*

Love foolishly

Get through the heartbreaks (if there be any)

Then love again,

Love hopelessly!

For only then can you declare that you know love as it should be known!

Love is air to your soul....

Your life is empty and dead without it.

Love is not free

It is invaluable and might cost you a lifetime.

Love is not enough.

Love makes music out of your life.

Love lives!

And like all living things, it requires to be nurtured..

Else it dies.

It is in the nature of love to grow

If it does not grow,

Then it is dying!

Love is not a game!

There are no losers or winners.

My Declaration

Despite what cards I have been dealt in life, today I choose to love! Not as I have been loved or not loved, but to love…the only way I alone can love another!

I do not decrease nor am I vulnerable in love, rather, love increases and will empower me to be the strongest I can be.

I refuse to hate or be caught up in the vicious cycle of regrets.

I choose to love every day, every one, everything, as best as I can. Though I may fail sometimes, tomorrow I arise and try again.

For my love is eternal, unwavering and unfailing in its zeal to express itself.

This makes my world a better place and my existence much more fulfilling!

My name is Dikachi Mann and I choose to #LOVE

Your

Declaration

My name is ....and

I choose tc #LOVE

About the author

Dikachi Mann is in his early thirties, an avid reader, a lover of life and all things beautiful. He currently works managing people. He loves to speak at events and travel the world.

He lives in Lagos, Nigeria and is currently concluding work on the third book in the LIVE, LOVE and LAUGH series.

www.ingramcontent.com/pod-product-compliance
Ingram Content Group UK Ltd.
Pitfield, Milton Keynes, MK11 3LW, UK
UKHW042001190726
13854UKWH00005B/2113

9 781523 476121